Especially for!
Josh + Kylie!
"Boo!"
Happy Trick-or-Treat!

Debra H. Ware

Nancy Robinson Masters

D1567439

THE *HORRIBLE* HOMEMADE HALLOWEEN COSTUME

BY

Nancy Robinson Masters

ILLUSTRATED BY

Debra H. Warr

MasAir Publications
4918 Newman Road
Abilene, TX 79601

Manufactured in Singapore by Tien Wah Press.

Produced by John R. Matthews, Inc.

An Ups and Downs Book

ISBN 0-9623563-3-6

For Walter

For Jeff and Alex

"We are going to have a Halloween party," Miss Parker said. "Everyone may wear a Halloween costume."

All the kids in Miss Parker's class clapped and cheered.

All the kids except me, Nancy Robinson.

I did not have a Halloween costume.

My dad was a cotton farmer during seven years of *drought*. A drought means it did not rain very much. Cotton plants need rain in order to grow.

As cotton plants grow they make round pods called *bolls*. Inside the boll are the fuzzy cotton fibers.

The fiber is pressed into large bales of smooth cotton. Farmers sell their bales of cotton to mills to be made into cloth.

"It hasn't rained on our farm all year," Daddy told us one morning. "We did not grow enough cotton bolls to make any bales to sell. All the cotton bolls we grew are in this sack."

He held the sack up with one hand. It looked like an enormous pillowcase. Printed on each side of the sack in black letters was "U.S.D.A."   That stands for United States Department of Agriculture.

"We won't have enough money to buy Halloween costumes this year," I heard him tell Mama.

A week before Halloween Miss Parker sent a note home with us to tell our parents about the Halloween party.

"Everyone should wear a Halloween costume," the note said.

"Oh, my," Mama said sadly. She was hanging towels out to dry on the clothesline when I handed the note to her.

Ker-plop!

The wind smacked a wet towel right in Mama's face.

"I know!" she said. She was smiling one of her special I've-got-an-idea smiles.

"Bring me that sack of cotton bolls," she told Daddy.

"Bring me two brown cotton towels from the bathroom cabinet," she told my always-tidy big sister.

"Bring me your glue," she told my always-making-messes big brother.

She spread the towels on the kitchen table.

Ker-plop! Ker-plop! Ker-plop!
Ker-plop! Ker-plop! Ker-plop!

Mama dabbed sticky blobs of glue all over the towels. To each sticky blob she stuck one of the cotton bolls!

She glued cotton bolls on her headscarf.

She glued cotton bolls on my socks.

She even glued cotton bolls on the United States Department of Agriculture sack.

"This sack will make the perfect trick-or-treat bag," she said.

"Ugh!" said my big sister.

"Neat!" said my big brother.

Mama sewed the two towels together on one end, leaving a small opening just large enough for my head in the middle. Then she sewed the sides together leaving an opening on each side for my arms.

"Homemade costumes are always the best kind," she said.

When the glue was almost dry she slid the two towels over my head.

She tied the headscarf under my hair.

She wrapped a piece of brown cloth around my waist for a belt.

"There!" she said. "You can go to the Halloween party dressed as a bale of cotton!"

Oh, my!

It was the most horrible, homemade Halloween costume I had ever imagined!

I waddled into the bedroom to look in the mirror. I had to hold my arms straight to keep them from being scratched by the dry, brown bolls.

Howler, the cat, gave a horrible howl.

"Ugly enough to make a train take a dirt road," I heard Daddy tell Mama.

Ker-plop. Ker-plop. Ker-plop.

There were tears as big as cotton bolls hitting my shoes. I tried to wipe my eyes with the headscarf but it was stuck to my hair.

"I don't want to be a bale of cotton," I wailed. "I want to be a fairy princess. Like this."

I showed Mama the picture of the fairy princess costume in last year's Christmas catalog. It had a pink lace top with a fluffy net skirt, and a magic wand that really sparkled!
All for the price of $9.98.

The pink ballerina slippers cost extra.

Fairy Princess Costu

Ker-plop. Ker-plop. Ker-plop.

Mama's tears sounded just like mine as they fell on the picture of the pink ballerina slippers.

"Oh, my," she said. "Maybe we can order these pink ballerina slippers next year."

I was so surprised I almost forgot to keep holding my arms straight.

I did not know Mama wanted to be a fairy princess for Halloween, too.

I stopped crying. If she could wait until next year to be a fairy princess, so could I.

When I peeked into our room at school there were catalog costumes everywhere.

Creepy pirates . . . frightful ghosts . . . scary cowboys . . . and *four* fairy princesses. All the fairy princesses were wearing pink ballerina slippers.

I was the only bale of cotton.

Ker-plop!

One of the cotton bolls came unglued and fell off !
I bent over to pick it up.

Ker-plop!

Another cotton boll rolled across the floor right in front of the
plastic pumpkin full of trick-or-treat candy by Miss Parker's desk.
All the fairy princesses started to laugh.

"Hey, look! Nancy's wearing *real* cotton bolls," one of the ghosts hollered from the back of the room.

"How did you get that cotton to stay in your hair?" one of the cowboys asked.

"You even *smell* like a bale of cotton," one of the pirates said.

I clutched my cotton sack and stood very, very still. I was afraid more cotton bolls might fall off if I moved.

"Well, you certainly *do* look like a bale of cotton," Miss Parker said. She was smiling just like Mama smiled when she made my homemade costume.

"Nancy may sit in my chair today so everyone can see what a *real* bale of cotton looks like."

The fairy princesses stopped laughing. Miss Parker had *never* let anyone sit in her chair before.

We spent the morning making orange paper pumpkins and reading spooky goblin stories. When it was time to get in line to walk to the cafeteria for lunch Miss Parker said, "Because Nancy is the *only* bale of cotton, she may be the leader."

All the fairy princesses tried to get in line right behind me.

"I'll trade you my wand for your sack," one of them whispered.

"No way," I told her.

Her wand did not have "U.S.D.A." printed on it like my sack did.

During the afternoon teachers from all the other classes asked Miss Parker if I could come to their room.

"We want everyone to see a bale of cotton," they said.

Before the last bell rang, the kids in Miss Parker's room voted for who should win First Prize and get the plastic pumpkin full of trick-or-treat candy.

Guess who won.

ME!

In my horrible, homemade Halloween costume!

I was so excited I ran all the way home. I could hardly wait to tell Mama she was right about a homemade Halloween costume being the very best kind.

Ker-plop! Ker-plop! Ker-plop!

I didn't even notice all the cotton bolls falling behind me as I ran.

When I saw the postman with his mailbag full of new Christmas catalogs to deliver, I stopped running.

Oh, my!

I was going to have to think of some way to tell Mama I did not want to be a fairy princess next year for Halloween.

Even though I *knew* she had her heart set
on both of us wearing pink ballerina slippers.

How To Make Your Own
HORRIBLE
HOMEMADE
HALLOWEEN COSTUME

1. Sew two cotton towels together on one end.
   Leave an opening in the middle large enough for your head.
   Sew the towels together on each side.
   Leave an opening on each side for your arms.

2. Use washable glue to stick things to the towels.

You could use two white cotton towels.
Glue red ribbon or crepe paper strips to the towels.
Be a gigantic candy cane!
(Don't forget to wrap some ribbon
   or crepe paper around your head!)

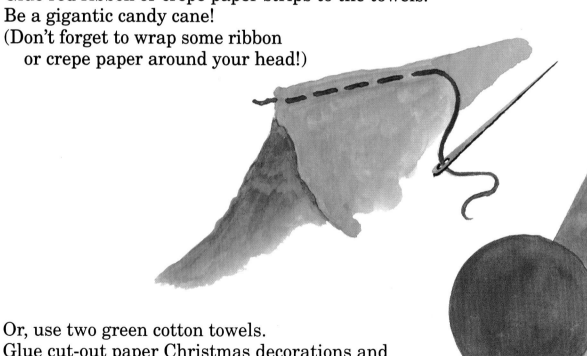

Or, use two green cotton towels.
Glue cut-out paper Christmas decorations and
   silver tinsel to the towels.
Be a Christmas tree!
(Don't forget to pin a star in your hair!)

Use two any color cotton towels.
Glue on popped popcorn and be a popcorn ball!
Glue on paper plates and be a flying saucer!
Glue on labels from canned foods and
be a bag of groceries!

You can have fun making your own horrible,
homemade Halloween costume *and*
help your family save money, too.
Remember, you can recycle your
costume.
Remove the stuff you glued on
and save the towels for next
year to make new costumes.

An Ups and Downs Book